It is only a little planet
But how beautiful it is.

ROBINSON JEFFERS

Celebrating the Earth is a series that reaches for rediscovery,
on the third planet from the sun, of the uniqueness there,
a uniqueness not only to celebrate, but also to savor.

There is but one ocean, although its coves have many names.
The single sea of atmosphere has no coves at all.
The miracle of soil, alive and giving life, lies thin
on the only earth, for which there is no spare.

In this series we seek a renewed stirring of love for that earth;
we plead that what man is capable of doing to it
is not always what he ought to do;
and we urge that all people now determine
that a wide spacious untrammeled freedom shall remain
to testify that this generation has love for the next.

Celebrating the Earth is about a different renaissance.
The old one came with discovery of new lands to exploit.
This new one comes with discovery of the earth's limits.

If, mindful of these limits, we learn new ways of perceiving
beauty and durability in the world, we may see that progress
is not the speed with which technology expands its control
or the rising number of things a man possesses,
but a process that lets man find serenity
and grow more content at less cost to the earth.

We shall welcome the inspiration of old masters and new.

DAVID R. BROWER

Only a little planet

Only a little planet

edited, with a foreword, by David R. Brower

lines by Lawrence Collins   photographs by Martin Schweitzer

FRIENDS OF THE EARTH · SAN FRANCISCO · NEW YORK · LONDON · PARIS · STOCKHOLM

HERDER AND HERDER · NEW YORK

If you go out at night
and look up you'll see
stars behind stars behind stars

and behind the smallest faintest stars
more night.

The stars are suns
like our sun
and all of them you can see
from the closest to the farthest
are a few, no more
of all the stars there are.

And all the black you see between them
a very thin slice of all
the black there is.

The planet you're standing on
looking out at the stars
is the earth, the third planet from the sun

and the mildest
and softest
of the nine.

It takes a year to go once
around the sun

and a day to spin once on its axis
the way a top spins.

In all the black you see
the only people we know
whose voices we can hear

the only animals we've seen
the only trees
the only insects, the only fish
we've ever seen

are here
hanging in nothing
the way a bubble
hangs in the air.

Solid and rocky and heavy
we think it is

when actually it's as pale and delicate and lovely
as a bubble.

It floats in nothing
with all of us on it
shining like a bubble.

Around it
water hangs, and
clouds sail, light comes down
in great sheets, and blocks
and tiny swirls like trails in water.

If you look up
in the daylight
the same sky is blue

or grey or green. The air
coloring

as it comes down. The earth
is brown or red or yellow

the sun pale white or yellow or orange
the water green then blue

then grey
with white foam rolling on its top, the trees

grass, bushes,
different greens.

If you try
to think both together

the blackness and the stars
and the close blue sky

it almost seems we move inside the bubble
as if it were a room with a fire
on a very cold night

and that if it burst

the cold would come rushing in
and hurt as much

as your brain can
looking farther and farther past
stars and stars
and black on top of black
until you have to think about something never ending
and can't.

The only trouble with thinking of it
as a living room
is that in a living room
you move things as you please.

The walls don't breathe
or the glasses you drink from, the floor is flat
and doesn't move

the rug doesn't grow
and the pictures on the wall
don't eat with you
at the table.

You do pretty much as you please
in a living room.

You can't do pretty much as you please
                              on the earth

not for long, anyway,
not unless you want the bubble to break

and the blackness
come pouring in

like black rain down a cold rainspout.

There's the earth
under your feet

and there's mist of green
and white
for clouds
and blue water.

There's the earth

with lives dreaming on it
sucking life in lonely places
fern valleys
and mountain lakes, forests, most of all the

green places
where life is thick.

Have you ever been in the woods
in a place where there were no
buildings
or roads

and the few flowers stood up alone out of
the undergrowth

not the way they do in gardens, in bunches.

A place where the sun is in pieces
through the leaves
like parts of a puzzle.

The light is stained the color
when it reaches the ground
of all the leaves it's been through.

In the tall forests like the deep redwood forests
the light gets so green and soft

you could almost swim in it
or splash it on your face
or pat it on like a soft powder.

A lot of people
haven't been there.
I never was
when I was young.

I lived in Brooklyn, in New York City.
There were trees on our block; oak, maple
and chestnut

but they stood in a row along the curb
not at all like the trees of the forest.

The chestnuts would fall and
we'd cut them out of their spiky skins
and make rings out of them
or throw them at each other.

The last time I saw the street I grew up on
the trees were gone. I wonder what it would be like now
to walk down to school and not be able to stop
for chestnuts or the seed pods from maples we'd stick
on our noses.

When you first stand in a deep forest
you notice first how quiet it is

then how much there is of everything
and how little
if you live in a city
you ever saw there.

It's like waking up the first morning of summer vacation
and realizing you don't have to go to school

don't have to go anywhere

and can take your time
about not going anywhere.

The trees rustle and talk
birds sit here and there
or rummage on the ground.

Water runs
and flowers stand up alone like signs saying
flower, what of it?

You get close to a fern
and see it's orange toward its center

get closer

and see the orange is ladybugs
hundreds of them.

A friend of mine
saw a bobcat

but I've never been that lucky.
Deer I've seen
and hawks, and a rattlesnake
and once an owl. It doesn't matter
which way you look

                               up or down
there's always something there.

You pull up
a mushroom
and break off its stem
and look closely
and there are hundreds of incredibly tiny insects

burrowing in and out
and hopping in its pores.

The little stream
has a garden snake drifting and rolling in it
his stripe wavering in the water.

In Stinson Beach in California
where I live now

a little horseshoe of a town half in the soft coast hills
half on sand
in front of the ocean

there's a snaking little trail that follows
a stream up the hill.

I walk it a lot
with my son who's four; he's been doing it
since he was two

so he climbs pretty well
for someone with short legs.

You pass the last house in town
and start up the path

covered over with laurel. It's like
a tunnel

                        green and shadowy.

It's narrow and steep.

Here there are more things alive
and you see more.

Newly born blind lizards
with orange bellies,
squirrels, snakes, birds
like drifting shadows,

airy water spiders
speeding on rocky pools,

things that move when you're almost
past them

trolls made of buckeye trunk

blue ghosts
made of sky
and bleached wood.

There's nothing there
that isn't alive

from the deadest fallen branch
to the water like running ice

everything

seems so much a part of everything else
nothing can be separated

                        or thought of as dead.

Most of California was alive
the way the trail is
not too long ago.

Probably there wasn't a single patch of the dead and ugly
anywhere
two hundred years ago.

We know more
about the dead and the ugly
than anyone alive then

know more about
how to make them.

One bulldozer could level
the trail I've been talking about.
Kill almost everything
so you'd never see life there again.

No hawks

no snakes

no trees

no ferns

no deer

no streams. Nothing but houses maybe
and concrete

and a few little shrubs on a lawn.

Someone might tell you that's progress
but I don't know.
Probably the man on the bulldozer would
or the man who hired the bulldozer
would call it that

but I don't know if you
would, if you went out to see a forest
full of animals and insects and running water
and what you saw was a house
and some concrete
and a mailbox.

You probably wouldn't.

They think because they leave the sky
and the horizon is still there
that everything is all right. They think
they're moving furniture around

mad housewives with earthmovers

and that nothing matters as long as the sky
is still there

and the horizon

and the two of them kind of sketch in
the earth.

But they say, you can't change the sky
with a bulldozer and a mailbox
and they believe it.

Because they don't notice
that a forest isn't a piece of furniture
or a deer a picture on the wall.

And all the time
as the ground gets more bare and they move in
the mailboxes

the air is getting strangely thin
and less nourishing.

And all the time the black and the cold
are building up out there
watching things die.

The dark can be soft
and come down softly
but on concrete
it comes down bang
and lies there.

And that's a different dark,
the dark of empty Mars

and frozen Pluto.

So don't believe them
when they say progress.

Think of the progress a bubble makes
as you blow it out bigger and bigger
and it breaks.

Believe them when you see a deer
nibbling a mailbox

or a hawk parking his car.

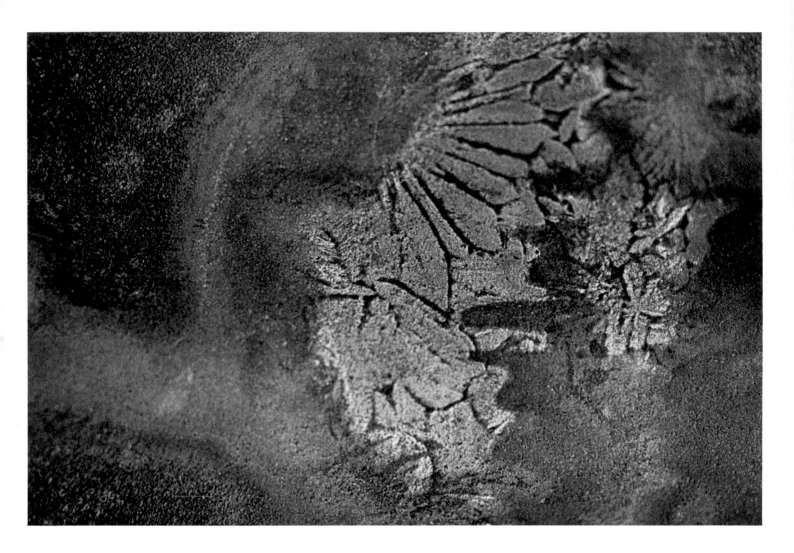

You won't. They have better things to do.

They don't look like us
and they don't think like us, and they're
                        all out there
looking and acting and thinking differently.

          Chipmunks, horses, cows,
          wombats, alligators, polar bears,
          whales, hummingbirds, my son, pigeons,

          I've seen these on the ground or in the water

          or the air.
          Fantastic whales with tails like driving
          crashing waves, tiny eyes in their huge bodies, bellies
          swirling through the green water

tiny eggbeater hummingbirds with shiny red throats
and fierce long beaks like lances

my little boy with strange sounds and words
and two-legged grime

bears with soft white backs

the horny claws of crocodiles
with bad joke smiles.

All these animals come
every bit of life on the planet
out of no more than a glass of seawater

tiny pushing circles in it of one-celled life
and elements and salts, air
and the incredible smoking blasts of prehistoric lightning

and even

with the millions of kinds of life there are
we find time to invent more in our heads

to spin out long green scaly dreams
                              with snaking fire breath

and white and golden one-horned horses.
Or we did
once, when we had

more wonder in our heads

and let it burst out
and make its own beasts.

Dragons and unicorns, phoenixes
and jabberwocks

centaurs, mermaids, trolls and gnomes
and flying horses. I've never seen one
but I know what they look like

never seen a living dinosaur
a tyrranosaurus say
but know what they look like from their giant
put-together bones in museums.

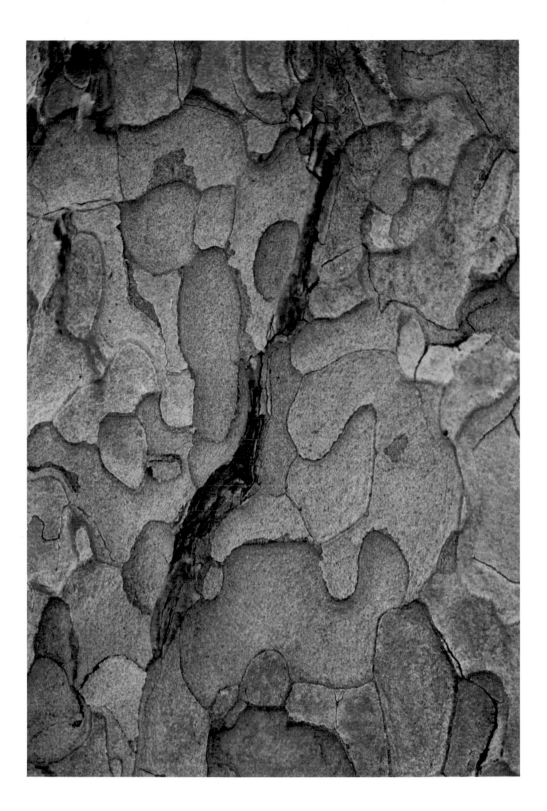

Imagine a real animal though
a dog, or a cat.

Now imagine the future
and the parents taking their children on a Sunday
to the museum to see piles of bones
labelled dog, cat, deer, or eagle.

The great grandchildren and the great great grandchildren
walking down the same concrete block
and up the same steps
to look at pictures and bones and try to imagine such a thing
in a backyard
or flying.

Imagine the great great great grand spawn
of things alive now who will never see us.

Imagine the time

the years

the slow changes

of one thing into another

                 and out again.

Imagine the lights of their eyes

as stars

and the years of their lives

as the distances between stars.

Imagine how long it took
to make a tiger.

Where the light comes from
in his eyes.

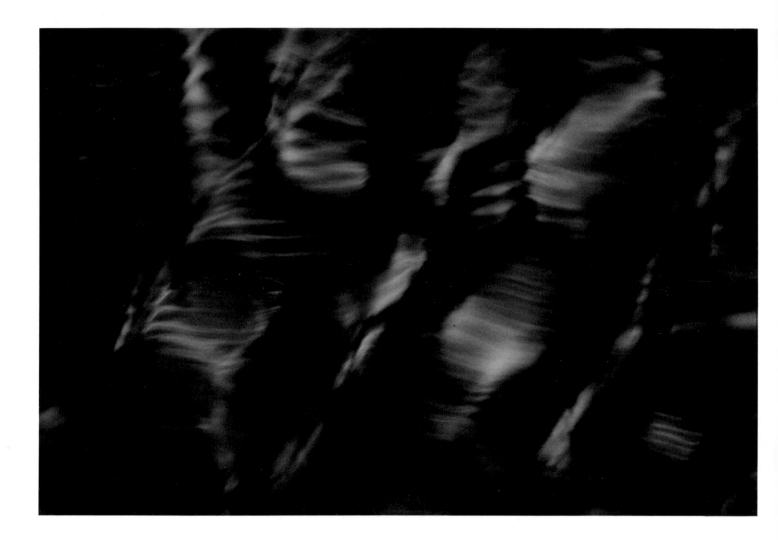

Every particle of every thing
rock, water, flower, human
has been in the same place flaming
in the heart of our ancient sun
before the earth
came flying out of it.

The irises in your eyes
the tissue of roses

the slow giant rocks in mountain hearts

were all born flaming
locked in the sun as it drifted
like a light on dark water.

Each of us sees
in a circle

and each of us is in a circle,
flowers swaying and touching
in the dark

passing from one to the other
the same circles, the same life

even the same particles
of flower
or flesh.

Circle within circle within circle
within blackness filled with circles

bumping
and spinning

being born
and dying

being
and moving.

If we let it

the earth can be born
again and again, facing the sun like those flowers
that open to the dawn
and close at night.

If we could see it all

together

on black space, nine planets, a sun

a bubble earth

with sweet air

water, rock, grass, lightning

butterflies

panthers

palm trees

maple syrup

milk

and ice

and branches

with strange shapes to them

beaches

where you dig and build

not caring

that the tide will fill

and wash away.

Our earth

colors of it
blackness

no color at all

silence in the forest, quick kinds of life
and slow redwood
dreaming kinds.

Water exploding

with thin tiny fine colored
lives

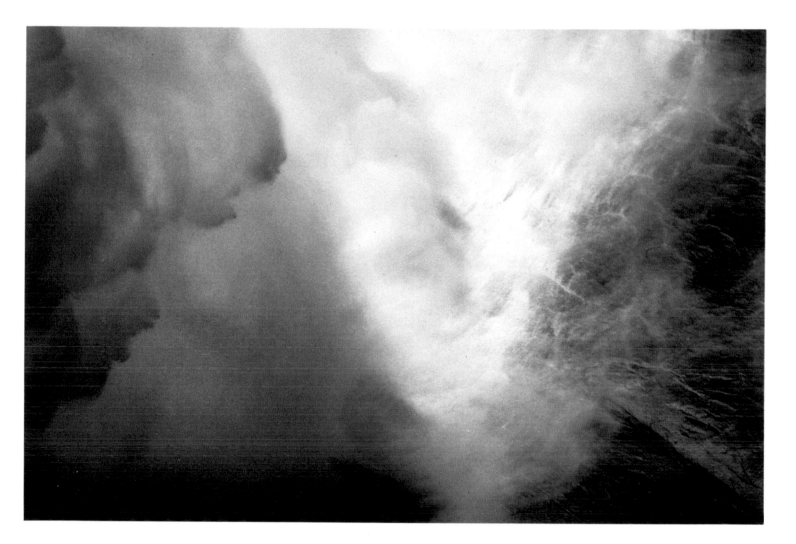

rain falling washing
banks of flowers, in
rain barrels, sounds of roofs and leaves

the giant fire
in an empty fireplace, the warm red dirt

the cold black rocks
with cool green lichen on them

other animals with strange eyes
seeing slanted or in only one or two colors

flicking their tongues or curling their tongues
or letting them out into flowers

if you can
just once

hold everything in your head.
Be able to look out your window
in the rain

and see everything.
Not just the rain, or the street, or the reflections
in the window

but everything at once.

See that the buildings are little blocks
and the grass and whatever trees there are
just perch on a little bit
of the very top of the ground

so that if you could unwind the earth
the way you can a baseball
they'd fall off and be gone
before you'd got past the first winding.

See that the rain doesn't seem to start or end
anywhere
just comes out of the air
and drops.

Notice that you breathe
in and out
and that the light in the sky changes all the time
in waves

and that the sky curves all the way around
to the edges of your eyes
then keeps going behind your head
to make a circle.

If you can feel the earth
under your feet

know that never
in your life
have you not been touching something

wearing it down a little
being worn down a little.

If you can stop, and let yourself look,
let your eyes do
what they do best,
stop
and let yourself see and see
that everything is doing things
to you
as you do things to everything.

Then you know
that although it is only a little planet
it is hugely beautiful
and surely the finest place in the world
to be.

So watch it, look at it
see what it's like
to walk around on it.

It's small but it's beautiful
it's small but it's fine
like a rainbow,

like a bubble.

Most of the photographs, which range from a Pacific cove to a rain-washed street just off Park Avenue, are details—partly by design and partly because that is the way they happened. I remember standing by a high glacial lake in the Sierra Nevada, twenty miles from the nearest road, watching a landscape of water, rock, and sky, all simple in their vastness. Then a glint of light sparkled through the grasses at the lake's edge, and I lay down and looked into a new world. Still smaller areas of color and texture led me to pause, marvel, and now and then to photograph, to try to fix a split second of a minute detail of the earth's voyage. The subtleties of light and weather, the happy accidents of things uniquely and briefly together, are always about us for the seeing. I am glad that the images in this book passed my way. Perhaps they will help you discover many more, and add other senses to what you see, even as the special sensing of Lawrence Collins has enriched what I saw.

MARTIN SCHWEITZER